MILTON AVERY

QUARRY POOL, 1951

milton avery

Introduction by Adelyn D. Breeskin

Published by THE NATIONAL COLLECTION OF FINE ARTS, SMITHSONIAN INSTITUTION

Distributed by THE NEW YORK GRAPHIC SOCIETY LTD., Greenwich, Connecticut 1969

Published by the National Collection of Fine Arts, Smithsonian Institution

Distributed by the New York Graphic Society Ltd.

Standard Book No. 8212-0348-7

Library of Congress Catalog Card No. 78-91440

Designed by Hubert Leckie

Printed in the Netherlands by Drukkerij de Lange/Van Leer N.V.

NATIONAL COLLECTION OF FINE ARTS
Smithsonian Institution
Washington, D.C.

December 12, 1969 through January 25, 1970

THE BROOKLYN MUSEUM
Brooklyn, New York

February 17 through March 29, 1970

THE COLUMBUS GALLERY OF FINE ARTS
Columbus, Ohio

April 24 through May 31, 1970

FOREWORD

THE SIGNIFICANT QUALITIES OF MILTON AVERY'S work became more apparent with each passing year, and the National Collection of Fine Arts has for some time planned to recognize this by presenting an exhibition extensive enough to allow an adequate assessment of his stature. Avery's apparently inexhaustible inventiveness in the simplest, most original terms of form and color can best be appreciated by bringing together a large number of his varied canvases. Despite Avery's importance, his work has never before been shown on such an extensive scale as in the present exhibition. The National Collection of Fine Arts is proud to be able to hold this large, comprehensive showing and to share it with the Brooklyn Museum and the Columbus Gallery of Fine Arts in order to give many people the opportunity to enjoy these paintings thoroughly.

We are profoundly grateful to Mrs. Milton Avery for her most generous help with so many loans. We are likewise grateful to Grace Borgenicht Brandt for lending a number of works from her gallery and from her private collection as well. Mr. Leslie Waddington of London is deserving of special thanks for having arranged for loans from English private collections as well as some from his gallery. Mr. Donald Morris of Detroit was very helpful also. We extend our gratitude to the private collectors who have deprived themselves of favorite paintings which grace the walls of their homes. To the museums and galleries among the lenders we extend our deep appreciation, realizing well the difficulties of making these loans.

In preparing the exhibition and the catalogue we wish to acknowledge the assistance of two staff members: Jan Keene Muhlert, assistant in the department of contemporary art, who prepared the biographical sketch and bibliography for the catalogue, and Abigail Booth, assistant curator of exhibits, for preparing the catalogue for publication.

Adelyn D. Breeskin
Curator of Contemporary Art
National Collection of Fine Arts

LENDERS TO THE EXHIBITION

Addison Gallery of American Art
Phillips Academy
Andover, Massachusetts

Edward Albee
New York, New York

Watkins Gallery
The American University
Washington, D.C.

Associated American Artists
New York, New York

Mrs. Milton Avery
New York, New York

The Baltimore Museum of Art
Baltimore, Maryland

Mrs. Robert M. Benjamin
New York, New York

Mr. and Mrs. S. O. Beren
Wichita, Kansas

Mr. and Mrs. Alex Bernstein
London, England

Mr. and Mrs. Cecil Bernstein
London, England

Mrs. Ruth M. Bernstein
Baltimore, Maryland

Mr. and Mrs. E. M. Black
New York, New York

Lawrence H. Bloedel
Williamstown, Massachusetts

Grace Borgenicht Gallery, Inc.
New York, New York

Mr. and Mrs. Nathan Borgenicht
Larchmont, New York

Mr. and Mrs. Warren Brandt
New York, New York

The Brooklyn Museum
Brooklyn, New York

Mr. and Mrs. Philip G. Cavanaugh
New York, New York

The Cleveland Museum of Art
Cleveland, Ohio

Mr. and Mrs. Wilfred P. Cohen
New York, New York

Mr. and Mrs. Keith Davis
Flint, Michigan

Dr. and Mrs. Hilbert H. DeLawter
Bloomfield Hills, Michigan

Mr. and Mrs. Henry G. Demant
Huntington Woods, Michigan

Mr. and Mrs. Charles Edward Eaton
Woodbury, Connecticut

Mr. and Mrs. Jerome A. Friedland
Detroit, Michigan

Mr. and Mrs. Richard Gray
Chicago, Illinois

Richard Gray Gallery
Chicago, Illinois

Mr. and Mrs. Ivor Green
Brooklyn, New York

Joseph H. Hirshhorn Foundation
New York, New York

Mr. and Mrs. Budd Hopkins
New York, New York

Jarvis Gallery
New York, New York

Mr. and Mrs. Richard L. Kanner
Huntington Woods, Michigan

Mr. and Mrs. Maury I. Kaplin
Toledo, Ohio

Tirca Karlis Gallery
Provincetown, Massachusetts

Mr. and Mrs. Louis Kaufman
Los Angeles, California

Kaye Kaz
New York, New York

Mr. and Mrs. Martin Kernerman
West Orange, New Jersey

Mr. and Mrs. Edward F. Kook
New York, New York

Mr. and Mrs. David Lloyd Kreeger
Washington, D.C.

Larivière Collection
Montreal, Canada

David Lebenbom
Detroit, Michigan

Mr. and Mrs. Bernard Livingston
New Rochelle, New York

Earle Ludgin
Chicago, Illinois

Mr. and Mrs. Richard H. Mandel
New York, New York

Dr. and Mrs. Sidney Merians
Edison, New Jersey

The Metropolitan Museum of Art
New York, New York

Mr. and Mrs. Donald Morris
Detroit, Michigan

Donald Morris Gallery, Inc.
Detroit, Michigan

Munson-Williams-Proctor Institute
Utica, New York

Museum of Fine Arts
Boston, Massachusetts

The Museum of Modern Art
New York, New York

National Collection of Fine Arts
Smithsonian Institution
Washington, D.C.

Roy R. Neuberger
New York, New York

The Phillips Collection
Washington, D.C.

Mr. and Mrs. Max J. Pincus
Pleasant Ridge, Michigan

Museum of Art
Rhode Island School of Design
Providence, Rhode Island

Dr. and Mrs. Harold Rifkin
Bronx, New York

Sheldon Ross
Detroit, Michigan

San Francisco Museum of Art
San Francisco, California

Santa Barbara Museum of Art
Santa Barbara, California

Dr. and Mrs. Stephen D. Senecoff
Detroit, Michigan

Mr. and Mrs. Joseph Shapiro
Oak Park, Illinois

John C. Stetson
Houston, Texas

Esther Stuttman
Washington, D.C.

University of Nebraska Art Galleries
Lincoln, Nebraska

Dr. and Mrs. Stanley M. Vickers
Huntington, New York

The Waddington Galleries
London, England

Wadsworth Atheneum
Hartford, Connecticut

Walker Art Center
Minneapolis, Minnesota

Mary Washington College
Fredericksburg, Virginia

Whitney Museum of American Art
New York, New York

Mrs. John Wintersteen
Philadelphia, Pennsylvania

Woodward Foundation
Washington, D.C.

INTRODUCTION

IN THESE DEEPLY TROUBLED TIMES it is a sustaining joy to look upon the works of Milton Avery and to find them so hearteningly beautiful. As the astronauts looked down on our earth and found it so alluring and lovely in contrast to the stark, deathlike surface of the moon, in similar fashion we may in this exhibition glory in Avery's fresh, lyrical, resplendent paintings as we compare them with much of the art now being produced that denies nature and reduces art to a minimum. Nature to Avery was a rich and endless feast of bountiful offerings for his eyes, which were attuned to translate everyday scenes into pure magic of color and form. Poetry and mystery abound in his vision of the world, finding expression with the effortless ease that only a master can achieve.

He developed a style of his own, with no predecessors whose work closely resembled his, and also with no direct followers. Many critics have compared his paintings to those of Albert Ryder. The comparison exists, I think, not in their finished works but rather in the aura surrounding their work and even in their viewpoints. For there is much mysticism in both of them. In *Paragraphs from the Studio of a Recluse* Ryder wrote: "It is the first vision that counts. The artist has only to remain true to this dream and it will possess his work in such a manner that it will resemble the work of no other man — for no two visions are alike."[1] These statements were as true of Avery as of Ryder. They both knew that it was the first vision that counted and that it had to possess them and remain vivid and true. Other statements by Ryder are equally applicable to Avery, for instance: "It is a wise artist who knows when to cry 'halt' in his composition, but it should be pondered over in his heart";[2] and again: "Art is long. The artist must buckle himself with infinite patience. His ears must be deaf to the clamor of his insistent friends who would quicken his pace. His eyes must see naught but the vision beyond. He must await the season of fruitage without haste, without worldly ambitions, without vexation of spirit."[3] All of this Avery upheld. He was always unhurried in his work and

he was patient. He did not start to sell his paintings to any extent until after 1950, and major exhibitions of his works were altogether too few throughout his lifetime.

The other artist to whom he is most often compared is Henri Matisse. The influence was in this case even more indirect, due much more to similarity of taste and temperament than to any intensive study of the French master's painting methods. Alfred Barr, in his great volume, *Matisse: His Art and His Public*, quotes a remark by Robert Motherwell: " 'Matisse may be the greatest living painter but I prefer Picasso; he deals with love and death.' To which [comments Mr. Barr] one might reply, on the same level, yes, but Matisse deals with love and life."[4] This is, indeed, a touchstone to the art of Matisse as well as to the art of Milton Avery. One can add to it Matisse's famous statement: "What I dream of is an art of balance, of purity and serenity devoid of troubling or depressing subject matter, an art which might be for every mental worker, be he businessman or writer, like an appeasing influence, like a mental soother, something like a good armchair in which to rest from physical fatigue."[5] His idea of comparing his art to an armchair has often been misunderstood. People are apt to think he meant that art demands no effort and is created without effort. But his own words refute this, as he has written: "I have always tried to hide my own efforts and wished my works to have the lightness and joyousness of a springtime which never lets anyone suspect the labors it has cost."[6]

It so happens that Milton Avery was a very silent man. He seldom spoke. He is known to have once remarked: "Why talk when you can paint?" But if he had talked or had written — which he also seldom did — he might very well have expressed exactly these same thoughts. They were, indeed, his thoughts concerning his work, and he upheld the same high ideals, expressing thorough satisfaction and contentment with his lot in life.

His paintings show his complete understanding not only of Matisse's guiding principles but also of his use of color as the mainspring of his art, and both artists treated figures and landscape primarily as patterns in harmonious arrangements. "To have the lightness and joyousness of a springtime which never lets anyone suspect the labors it has cost" – that, too, was the aim of Avery as he worked to eliminate and to simplify more and more. Both artists visualized their compositions from the start and considered first of all the overall expression. To both of them composition was the art of arranging in a decorative manner the different elements chosen to express their feeling. Above all, color was to be expressive, the choice of colors being intuitive, not based on any color theories or charts. Matisse's palette was much the brighter, the more intense. Avery's color is apt to be more calm, more muted, with fewer brilliant accents. His is a less complex art but through the years it has proven to be strongly assertive, as the American equivalent of the best European art tradition of the earlier years of this century. His approach was foreign to most American artists of the 30s and 40s. We must now recognize, therefore, that his work was one of the main channels through which such important principles, handed down through the great classical tradition in France, were upheld and nurtured in our country even though Avery never studied abroad and did not even visit there until the summer of 1952.

He always went his own artistic way, keeping his own counsel and maintaining his equilibrium in the face of such rampant proselytizing as was engaged in by Thomas Craven and the American Scene painters to eliminate any influences from overseas. Thomas Benton, Craven's close cohort, wrote at that time: "The fact that our art was arguable in the language of the street . . . was proof to us that we had succeeded in separating it from the hothouse atmospheres of an imported and, for our country, functionless aesthetics. With that proof we felt that we were on the way to releasing American art from its subservience to borrowed forms."[7] In trying, quite blatantly with pumped-up propaganda, to create an art that was 100 per cent American they lost a sense of quality and veered toward commercial illustration. But Avery pursued a very different course, advancing steadily and consistently through the 50s and reaching his peak near the end of his life with his best works of the early 60s his very finest.

He was always completely loyal to his own sensibilities, unswerving, never tempted by changing fads or "isms." He preserved a certain innocence, which was maintained in spite of experience which brought with it a rare kind of sophistication – a sophistication evidenced in his art rather than within himself. His understanding of method, of techniques, of color was thoroughly pervasive. A great teacher, Hans Hofmann, was moved to say that Avery was one of the first to understand color as a creative means. He knew how to relate colors in a plastic way. His color actually achieves a life of its own, sometimes lovely and gentle, at other times startlingly tart, yet always subtle and eloquent.

One of Avery's rarest attributes was his keen sense of humor. Edwin Mullins in *The London Magazine* of January 1965 wrote: "Laughter is as fundamental in an Avery as *angst* is in a Kirchner, fear in a Munch, pomposity in a Reynolds and sex in a Modigliani."[8] There is something completely disarming in Avery's humor. It is always good-natured, never sardonic. We find it at its most engaging in his many self-portraits, for example *Avery on 57th Street* [no. 21]. They are amusing and light-hearted and also very well painted. *Rooster's Domain* [no. 46] is another of his paintings over which he must have chuckled as he worked, as well as *Bicycle Rider by the Loire* [no. 69]. This sense of humor was an endearing quality which helped to win many friends for him.

In New York he was close to both Mark Rothko and Adolph Gottlieb, and both admired him as an artist and were devoted to him personally. They were about ten years his junior but the three of them criticized each other's work and encouraged each other to good purpose. Although both Rothko and Gottlieb gradually grew more and more abstract, they were closer in their general approach to Avery than they were to action painters such as Pollock and de Kooning. Rothko, especially, has preserved a sense of weightless suspension in his monumental canvases which also marks many of Avery's later works. He feels that Avery was unique in being able to express the human quality so directly, with no false attributes, and realizes that for him his maintenance of the human image was right.

In reminiscing on their earlier years together, Gottlieb has mentioned what a wonderful draughtsman Avery was. In his drawings the figures were more literal than they would appear later in the paintings which developed from the sketches. In them there was a realism of a sort, with distortion accentuating what was characterstic in the model or giving play to the humor that was so characteristic of Avery. Heads might be reduced in size, figures be elongated, or thighs be exaggerated, but the pose was always fully expressed. From such sketches he blocked in his paintings of figures, simplifying the contours, flattening the masses, purifying and refining and articulating the image with a structural simplicity that defies description. His aim was to present exact gesture and exact feeling within a very strictly limited design. Then with color he added emotion and very often surprise – due to unexpected accents and off-beat colors. Edwin Mullins in his article mentioned above comments: "With Avery . . . the gift of being a great colourist is not a matter of selecting beautiful colours . . . but rather of selecting a range of colours which cohere and complement each other like notes in a chosen key . . . if it were possible to weigh against each other the different areas of colour with which Avery builds up a single painting, they would be found to be more or less equal... Their uniform lightness of tone . . . emphasises the flatness of the paint-surface, and emphasises too that the artist's concern is with the purely surface qualities of a subject, not with its density and volumes."[9]

It is this awareness of surface that allies him definitely with the dominant modern American school. He looked at nature as a substance of surface alone, accessible wholly through his eyes, by means of which he recorded on canvas rare, rich moments of deep perception and gave them permanence. On looking at his powerful landscapes and shorescapes we sense the truth of his vision as well as the beauty of his feeling. In these he comes closest to sheer abstraction with remarkably well controlled color and extremely simplified compositions. The dominant horizontal of the horizon line offered a stabilizing sense of quietude, whereas for a sense of contrasting movement he would sometimes introduce patterns of zigzags or scumbled paint in ripples or dashes. Finally, as he flattened his canvases more and more, abstraction took over completely in such paintings as *Green Sea* [no. 70], *Black Sea* [no. 98], or *Sand, Sea and Sky* [no. 100].

Many important elements of his art were formed early in his career and some characteristics were even bred in his bones, such as his New England reticence and his Yankee dryness of wit and humor. Therefore some basic facts regarding his life are in order. He was born in Altmar, in Upper New York State not far from Oswego, where his father was a farmer. When he was eight years old, his family moved to Hartford, Connecticut, where he grew up in a New England atmosphere – a quiet boy, never given much to conversation or boisterous activity. When about eighteen he took a correspondence course in lettering, having decided to become a commercial artist. He then enrolled at the Connecticut League of Art Students but upon finding that the class in lettering was full, he was persuaded to join the life class. The teacher was Charles Noel Flagg, who was unable to fire him with any enthusiasm. Consequently he left, and it can certainly be said that he became a self-taught artist. In order to be able to paint during the daytime, mostly sketching out in the open, he took a night job and continued working under such an arrangement for a number of years.

In the summer of 1925 he went to Gloucester to join the artists' colony and there met Sally Michel, from Brooklyn, who had also come for a summer of painting. In the fall he followed her to New York and in the spring of the next year they were married. Few marriages have been so auspicious. Milton was able to devote his full time to painting, since Sally was a remarkable provider. Even during the Depression she was able to hold an illustrating job which gave them a livelihood. In 1932 their daughter March was born – a lovely daughter painted so often by her father that he had an exhibition at Durand-Ruel in New York in 1947 of paintings just of March. Their family life provided him with most of his subjects other than his landscapes, seascapes and a few portraits of friends.

Throughout the 30s the artist was assimilating his artistic vocabulary. His mood was gay, his course laid out without any deviation – direct and seemingly untroubled. During the Depression the going was rough and there were few sales, but he was highly respected by his fellow artists and had many friends who would gather in the Averys' big, one-room apartment in Lincoln Square, not to buy but to talk and to look at Milton's pantings. Later the Averys lived on West 11th Street in a pleasant apartment where Milton painted in the main living room throughout the winter months. Across from his easel there was a big Cape Cod rocking chair and there he would sit, rocking back and forth while considering and mulling over his painting. When visitors came to see Milton's paintings it was Sally who received them, who did all of the talking for them both, and who pulled out the paintings from their neatly stacked bins, while Milton sat in his chair and every once in a while would interject a humorous quip or a word or so relating to a special work. In the early 50s he was quite seriously ill and after that remained somewhat fragile so that handling the paintings was usually left to Sally.

During the summer the family went to Gloucester, to Cape Ann or some other New England seaside place where Milton covered page after page of rather small notebooks with sketches – many of them very summary with color notations jotted down. From them somewhat larger watercolors were developed and from these the oil paintings gradually were completed. By this procedure his work was refined, his color carefully selected and applied. He modified and strengthened his sketches and wove them into a strictly articulated design, becoming always more simple and more sensitively attuned through his relaxed and reposeful temperament, as he thought them through while sitting in his rocking chair.

Once a week he attended a sketch class in New York's Greenwich Village, drawing from the model, and continued this custom throughout most of his career. He found that it was splendid practice in the exact formulation of the visual expression. The gesture and feeling of the pose were set down economically in as truthful a statement as was possible. He later favored a felt-tipped pen and wielded it with great speed after studying the model thoroughly. He was always faithful to his own vision and steadfast in his judgments. Also he was wholly American in the same way that Homer, Ryder and Eakins were American. His love of the sea he had in common with the first two, whereas he shared with Eakins a deep sense of truth. He was as courageous as they were. Each held to his own characteristic way of seeing, regardless of outside influences.

To expatiate further upon Avery's art would be, for me, redundant. Having known him as a most congenial, delightful and charming friend, I would prefer to let others with more perspective now give their varied opinions of his art. There is Mr. Norman Reid, director of the Tate Gallery in London, where Avery has found a most enthusiastic reception, who has written:

> London has been fortunate in seeing four Milton Avery exhibitions in the last six years, presented by the Waddington Galleries with a restraint and clarity appropriate to his work. Appreciation of his vision – quiet, lyrical and observant, but also anticipatory in its formal simplifications, thinned paint textures and resonant colours – has steadily grown in Britain. The Tate Gallery's own large Avery, *Yellow Sky* 1958, a most welcome gift in 1963, has a distinguished position in the Gallery's developing collection of major postwar American art.[10]

Clement Greenberg, eminent critic, wrote in 1958 and

included in his book of essays *Art and Culture* the following words:

> It is difficult to account for the individuality of Avery's art... There is the sublime lightness of Avery's hand on the one side, and the morality of his eyes on the other: The exact loyalty of these eyes to what they experience. The question has to do with *exactly* how Avery locks his flat, lambent planes together; with the *exact* dosage of light in his colors (all of which seem to have some admixture of white): with *exactly* how he manages to keep his pictures cool in key even when using the warmest hues; with *exactly* how he inflects planes into depth without shading, and so on. Of course, all successful art confronts us with this factor of exactness, but rarely does the necessity of exactness cover as much as it does in Avery's case.[11]

One of the very few books on Avery so far published is *Milton Avery Paintings 1930-1960* by Hilton Kramer. In it Mr. Kramer pays fine tribute to Avery, and among its many incisive statements he writes:

> There is scarcely a more refined aesthetic intelligence in American art than his... In the deployment of painterly forms, in the whole expressive and logistic enterprise of handling the materials of painting, Avery has been equaled by very few of his contemporaries; but an absorption in such problems has never been a primary characteristic of his art. What he saw in French art, what he particularly valued, and what has interested him ever since, was a *vision* that cast some light on his own emotions and helped provide him with a syntax for his own mode of feeling. ... The work of a painter of Avery's constancy inevitably takes on new meanings with the passage of time ... In the perspective from which we are now able to view Avery's development, his originality is clearer. The order and delicacy of his mind are more powerful than one had been led to expect. His sensibility, which from the start has been notable for its sweetness and good-humored elegance, may now be seen as the subtlest in the American art of our time.[12]

In a 1968 article in *The New York Times* Mr. Kramer wrote:

> The late Milton Avery was a painter of extraordinary accomplishment. He was one of the finest landscape painters to have emerged on the American art scene in this century. He was also a colorist of genius.[13]

Henry Geldzahler in *American Painting in the Twentieth Century* wrote:

> Avery's directness in color and his simplicity of form do not in any way reduce the complexity or variety of his work. It is this, as much as anything in his painting, that has served as a lesson to the younger abstractionists.[14]

James R. Mellow writing in *Art International* in 1968:

> Avery created one of the most remarkable oeuvres in American art. That his work held firmly to recognizable subject-matter, to certain aspects of the American scene, when American art was developing its own authoritative forms of abstraction, is part of its uniqueness.[15]

And finally, there is the memorial address delivered by Avery's fellow artist and close friend, Mark Rothko, at the New York Society for Ethical Culture on January 7, 1965. We are grateful to Mr. Rothko for the privilege of reprinting his remarks in their entirety on the following page.

Adelyn D. Breeskin

1 Albert Pinkham Ryder, "Paragraphs from the Studio of a Recluse," in *American Art, 1700-1960, Sources and Documents*, John W. McCoubrey, ed., Englewood Cliffs, New Jersey, 1965, p. 187.

2 Ibid.

3 Ibid.

4 Alfred H. Barr, Jr., *Matisse: His Art and His Public*, New York, 1966, p. 266.

5 Ibid., p. 122.

6 Matisse to Henry Clifford, February 14, 1948, in *Henri Matisse*, Philadelphia Museum of Art, 1948, p. 15.

7 Thomas Hart Benton, "On Regionalism," *American Art, 1700-1960, Sources and Documents*, p. 202.

8 Edwin Mullins, "Milton Avery," *The London Magazine*, vol. 4 (January 1965), p. 40.

9 Ibid., p. 36.

10 Letter to the author, December 10, 1968.

11 Clement Greenberg, *Art and Culture*, pp. 199-200.

12 Hilton Kramer, *Milton Avery: Paintings 1930-1960*, p. 11.

13 Hilton Kramer, "Art: For Eye and Spirit," *The New York Times*, May 11, 1968, p. 34M.

14 Henry Geldzahler, *American Painting in the Twentieth Century*, p. 173.

15 James R. Mellow, "A Note on Milton Avery," *Art International*, vol. 12 (October 20, 1968), p. 62.

COMMEMORATIVE ESSAY

I would like to say a few words about the greatness of Milton Avery.

This conviction of greatness, the feeling that one was in the presence of great events, was immediate on encountering his work. It was true for many of us who were younger, questioning, and looking for an anchor. This conviction has never faltered. It has persisted, and has been reinforced through the passing decades and the passing fashions.

I cannot tell you what it meant for us during those early years to be made welcome in those memorable studios on Broadway, 72nd Street, and Columbus Avenue. We were, there, both the subjects of his paintings and his idolatrous audience. The walls were always covered with an endless and changing array of poetry and light.

The instruction, the example, the nearness in the flesh of this marvelous man — all this was a significant fact — one which I shall never forget.

Avery is first a great poet. His is the poetry of sheer loveliness, of sheer beauty. Thanks to him this kind of poetry has been able to survive in our time.

This — alone — took great courage in a generation which felt that it could be heard only through clamor, force and a show of power. But Avery had that inner power in which gentleness and silence proved more audible and poignant.

From the beginning there was nothing tentative about Avery. He always had that naturalness, that exactness and that inevitable completeness which can be achieved only by those gifted with magical means, by those born to sing.

There have been several others in our generation who have celebrated the world around them, but none with that inevitability where the poetry penetrated every pore of the canvas to the very last touch of the brush. For Avery was a great poet-inventor who had invented sonorities never seen nor heard before. From these we have learned much and will learn more for a long time to come.

What was Avery's repertoire? His living room, Central Park, his wife Sally, his daughter March, the beaches and mountains where they summered; cows, fish heads, the flight of birds; his friends and whatever world strayed through his studio: a domestic, unheroic cast. But from these there have been fashioned great canvases, that far from the casual and transitory implications of the subjects, have always a gripping lyricism, and often achieve the permanence and monumentality of Egypt.

I grieve for the loss of this great man. I rejoice for what he has left us.

Mark Rothko

January 7, 1965

MARK ROTHKO, 1933

POETRY READING, 1957

DARK FOREST, 1958

SEA GRASSES AND BLUE SEA, 1958

SPRING ORCHARD, 1959

TANGERINE MOON AND WINE DARK SEA, 1959

BEACH BLANKETS, 1960

DUNES AND SEA II, 1960

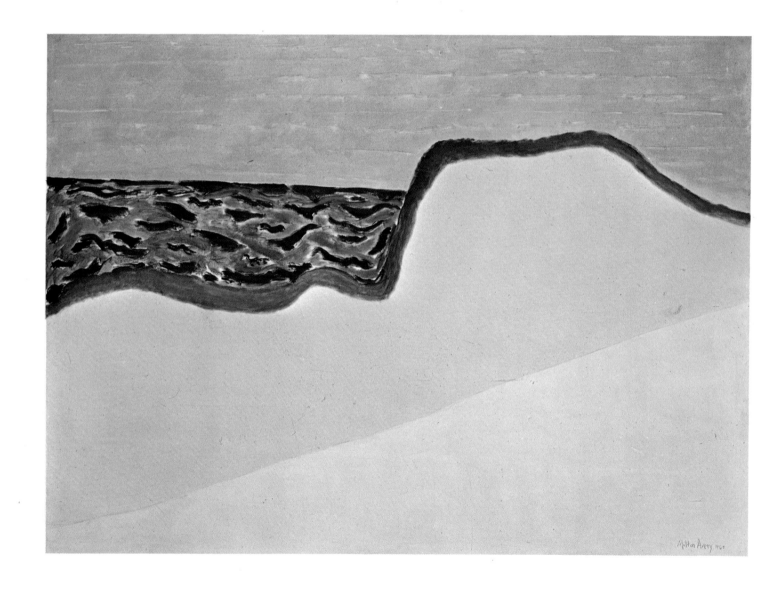

PLUNGING GULL, 1960

1 SUNDAY RIDERS, 1929

oil, 30 x 25
Lent by Roy R. Neuberger

CATALOGUE OF
THE EXHIBITION

Dimensions are in inches; height precedes width.

Oil paintings are on canvas unless otherwise noted.

2 SELF PORTRAIT, 1930
 oil, 19¼ x 15½
 Lent by University of Nebraska Art Galleries,
 Howard S. Wilson Memorial Collection

3 SLEEPING GIRL, 1930
 ink, 11 x 14
 Lent anonymously

4 WOMAN WITH MANDOLIN, 1930
 oil, 33½ x 24½
 Lent by Dr. and Mrs. Harold Rifkin

5 HARBOR AT NIGHT, 1932
oil, 32 x 48
Lent by The Phillips Collection
(exhibited in Washington only)

7 SITTERS BY THE SEA, 1933
oil, 28 x 36
Lent by Mrs. Milton Avery

MARK ROTHKO, 1933
oil, 22½ x 16
Lent by Museum of Art,
Rhode Island School of Design,
The Albert Pilavin Memorial Collection
(exhibited in Washington only)

8 MY WIFE, SALLY, 1934
drypoint, 5½ x 8¼
Lent by Associated American Artists

9 RIDERS IN THE PARK, 1934
drypoint, 3¹⁵⁄₁₆ x 4⅞
Lent by Associated American Artists

10 LITTLE GIRL, 1936
oil, 36 x 24
Lent by Philip G. Cavanaugh

11 ROTHKO WITH PIPE, 1936
etching, 7 3/16 x 6 3/4
Lent by National Collection of Fine Arts,
Smithsonian Institution

13 SALLY WITH BERET, 1939
drypoint, 8 x 6 5/16
Lent by Associated American Artists

12 GULLS, GASPE, 1938

oil, 30 x 40
Lent by Addison Gallery of American Art,
Phillips Academy

14 BASKET OF FISH, 1940

oil, 30 x 34
Lent by Mr. and Mrs. Wilfred P. Cohen

15 THE BROWN HAT, circa 1941
   oil, 36 x 28
   Lent by Mr. and Mrs. Edward F. Kook

16 LITTLE GIRL, circa 1941
   gouache, 20 x 14
   Lent by Kaye Kaz

17 SELF PORTRAIT, 1941
oil, 54 x 34
Lent by Roy R. Neuberger

18 ARTIST'S DAUGHTER, 1942
watercolor, 30 x 22
Lent by Mr. and Mrs. Ivor Green

19 PORTRAIT OF EILSHEMIUS, 1942
  oil, 36 x 28
  Lent by Mr. and Mrs. Louis Kaufman

21 AVERY ON 57th STREET, 1943
  oil, 36 x 28
  Lent by Tirca Karlis Gallery
  (exhibited in Washington and Brooklyn only)

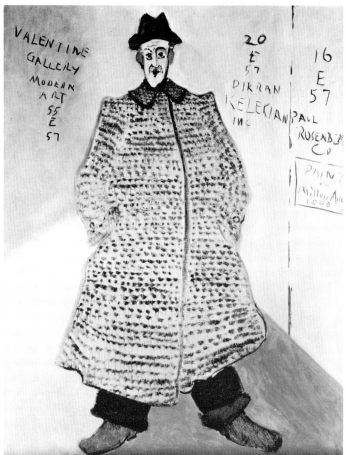

20 GASPE LANDSCAPE, 1942/43
oil, 36 x 48
Lent by Roy R. Neuberger

22 THE PINK COCK, 1943
oil, 36 x 48
Lent by Earle Ludgin

23 PORTRAIT OF MARSDEN HARTLEY, 1943
oil, 36 x 28
Lent by Museum of Fine Arts, Boston,
Charles Henry Hayden Fund

24 FENCERS, 1944
oil, 48 x 32
Lent by Santa Barbara Museum of Art,
Gift of Mrs. Burton G. Tremaine

25 THE PINK TABLECLOTH, 1944
oil, 32⅛ x 48⅛
Lent by Munson-Williams-Proctor Institute,
Gift of Mr. and Mrs. Roy R. Neuberger

26 SEATED GIRL WITH DOG, 1944
oil, 44 x 32
Lent by Roy R. Neuberger

27 STILL LIFE WITH DERBY, 1944
 oil, 28 x 36
 Lent by Roy R. Neuberger

28 TWO FIGURES AT A DESK, 1944
 oil, 48 x 32
 Lent by Roy R. Neuberger

29 YELLOW MOONLIGHT, 1944
gouache, 22 x 30
Lent by Mrs. John Wintersteen

30 ARTIST'S WIFE, 1945
oil, 30 x 25
Lent by Mr. and Mrs. Max J. Pincus

31 CARD PLAYERS, 1945
oil, 50 x 34
Lent by Jarvis Gallery

32 GEORGE CONSTANT FISHING, 1945
watercolor, 20 x 30
Lent by Mr. and Mrs. Charles Edward Eaton

33 GREEN LANDSCAPE, 1945

oil, 56 x 46
Lent by Watkins Gallery,
The American University

34 HUSBAND AND WIFE, 1945

oil, 33¾ x 44
Lent by Wadsworth Atheneum

35 ROCKY COVE, 1945
  watercolor, 22 x 30
  Lent by Dr. and Mrs. Stephen D. Senecoff

36 SEASIDE WATCHERS, 1945
  watercolor, 22 x 30
  Lent anonymously

37 STUDIOUS SKETCHER, 1945
   oil, 36 x 28
   Lent by The Cleveland Museum of Art,
   Contemporary Collection
   (exhibited in Washington and Brooklyn only)

38 MORNING CALL, 1946
   oil, 54 x 34
   Lent by Joseph H. Hirshhorn Foundation

39 NUDE SEATED, 1946
oil, 32½ x 26½
Lent by Mr. and Mrs. Martin Kernerman

40 SEATED BLONDE, 1946
oil, 52 x 34
Lent by Walker Art Center

41 WHITE FACE, 1950
monotype, 23½ x 17⅞
Lent by Associated American Artists

42 WHITE SEA, 1947
oil, 30 x 40
Lent by Mr. and Mrs. Warren Brandt

43 AUTUMN SEA, 1948
watercolor, 22 x 30
Lent by Mr. and Mrs. Richard H. Mandel

44 GREEN SEA, 1948
watercolor, 22 x 30
Lent by Mr. and Mrs. Keith Davis

45 ORANGE ROCKS, 1948
oil, 30 x 40
Lent by Mr. and Mrs. E. M. Black

46 ROOSTER'S DOMAIN, 1948
  oil, 30 x 40
  Lent by Roy R. Neuberger

48 MARCH IN RED, 1950
  oil, 42 x 26
  Lent by Sheldon Ross and David Lebenbom

47 SELF PORTRAIT, 1949
  oil on board, 20 x 16
  Lent by John C. Stetson

49 MATERNITY, 1950

oil, 32 x 46
Lent by Mrs. Milton Avery

51 RECLINING NUDE, 1950

felt-tipped pen, 14 x 17
Lent by Mr. and Mrs. Joseph Shapiro

50 RECLINING BATHERS, 1950

monotype, 17 x 22
Lent by Mr. and Mrs. Maury I. Kaplin

52 SUMMER READER, 1950
  oil, 34 x 44
  Lent by Mrs. Ruth M. Bernstein

53 THREE FIGURES, 1950
  felt-tipped pen, 13½ x 16½
  Lent by Mr. and Mrs. Budd Hopkins

54 WHITE AND GREY NUDE, 1950
oil, 36 x 28
Lent by Mr. and Mrs. Richard L. Kanner

55 BLACK GOAT, WHITE GOAT, 1951
oil, 34 x 38
Lent by Mr. and Mrs. Max J. Pincus

58 QUARRY POOL, 1951
oil, 28 x 36
Lent by The Waddington Galleries

56 CLEAR CUT LANDSCAPE, 1951
oil, 31 x 43½
Lent by San Francisco Museum of Art,
Gift of the Women's Board

57 PALE FLOWER, 1951 ?
oil, 30 x 40
Lent by Mr. and Mrs. Warren Brandt

59 BREAKING SEA, 1952
oil, 30 x 40
Lent by The Baltimore Museum of Art,
Frederic Cone Fund for Contemporary American Art

60 MOUNTAIN LAKE, 1952
oil, 28 x 36
Lent by Mr. and Mrs. Richard Gray

62 SUNSET, 1952
oil, 42 x 48
Lent by The Brooklyn Museum,
Gift of Roy R. and Marie S. Neuberger Foundation, Inc.

61 SHEEP, 1952
oil, 30 x 40
Lent by Mrs. Milton Avery

63 ABALONE SHELL, 1953
oil, 34 x 39
Lent anonymously

64 ADVANCING SEA, 1953
   oil, 40 x 46
   Lent by Mrs. Milton Avery

65 DARK ROAD, 1953
   watercolor, 22 x 30
   Lent by Mr. and Mrs. Henry G. Demant

66 DIEPPE, 1953
oil, 28 x 36
Lent by Mr. and Mrs. Keith Davis

68 THE SEINE, 1953
oil, 41 x 50
Lent by Whitney Museum of American Art

67 LANDSCAPE WITH TREES, 1953
oil, 29 x 36
Lent by Richard Gray Gallery

69 BICYCLE RIDER BY THE LOIRE, 1954
oil, 38 x 55
Lent by Mr. and Mrs. Keith Davis

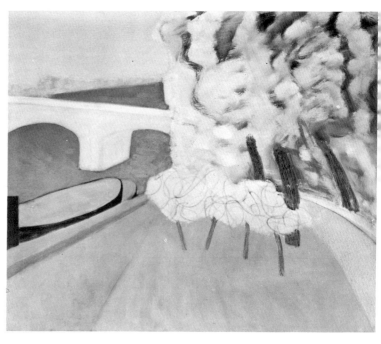

70 GREEN SEA, 1954

oil, 42 x 60
Lent by The Metropolitan Museum of Art,
Arthur H. Hearn Fund, 1954

72 PINK PASTURE, 1954

oil, 30 x 39¾
Lent by Mary Washington College

71 MARCH IN BROWN, 1954

oil, 44 x 32
Lent by Mr. and Mrs. Philip G. Cavanaugh

73 TREES BY LITTLE POND, 1954

watercolor. 22 x 30
Lent by Mr. and Mrs. Nathan Borgenicht

74 WATERFALL, 1954

oil, 32 x 52
Lent by Roy R. Neuberger

75 WHITE NUDE, 1954
   oil 36 x 57
   Lent anonymously

76 MORNING SEA, 1955
   oil. 38 x 56
   Lent anonymously

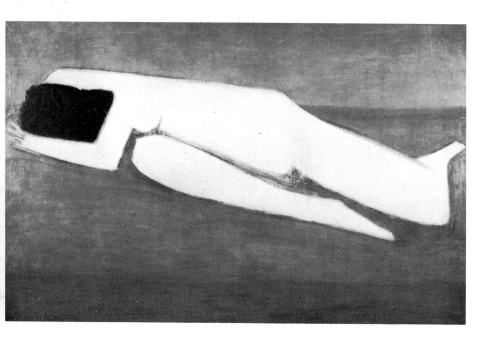

77 SARATOGA LAKE, 1955

oil, 40 x 46
Lent anonymously

78 UPPER PASTURE, 1955

oil, 46 x 52
Lent by Mr. and Mrs. Cecil Bernstein

79 NUDE ON CHAIR, 1956

ink, 17 x 14
Lent by Mrs. Robert M. Benjamin

80 NUDE WITH RED DRAPE, 1956
oil, 44 x 32
Lent by National Collection of Fine Arts,
Smithsonian Institution,
Gift of John Henry Berne

81 SEA GAZERS, 1956
oil, 30 x 44
Lent by Lawrence H. Bloedel

82 SOLITARY TREE, 1956
monotype, 23½ x 17⅞
Lent by Associated American Artists

83 VICTORIAN STILL LIFE, 1956

oil, 32 x 38
Lent by Edward Albee
(exhibited in Washington and Brooklyn only)

84 LONE GULL, 1957

oil, 36 x 18
Lent anonymously

85 POETRY READING, 1957
oil, 43¾ x 56
Lent by Munson-Williams-Proctor Institute

86 SPEEDBOAT'S WAKE, 1957
watercolor, 20 x 26
Lent by Dr. and Mrs. Stanley M. Vickers

87 WHITE MOON, 1957
oil, 50 x 38
Lent by Esther Stuttman

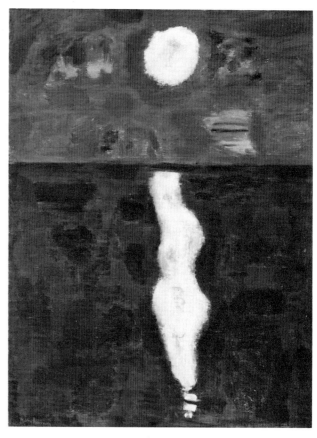

88 ANEMONES, 1958

oil on canvas board, 28 x 22
Lent by Lawrence H. Bloedel

90 DARK FOREST, 1958

oil, 40 x 53
Lent by Mr. and Mrs. Donald Morris

89 DARK DUNE, 1958

felt-tipped pen, 6¼ x 10⅝
Lent by National Collection of Fine Arts,
Smithsonian Institution

91 DUNE BUSHES, 1958
   oil, 54 x 72
   Lent anonymously

92 DUNE GRASSES, 1958

felt-tipped pen, 8½ x 11
Lent by Mr. and Mrs. Philip G. Cavanaugh

93 HOT MOON, 1958

oil, 54 x 66½
Lent by Larivière Collection

94 SEA AND DUNE I, 1958

oil, 54 x 72
Lent anonymously

95 SEA GRASSES AND BLUE SEA, 1958

oil, 60⅛ x 72⅜
Lent by The Museum of Modern Art,
Gift of friends of the artist, 1959

96 SUNSET ON A QUIET SEA, 1958

oil, 48 x 72
Lent anonymously

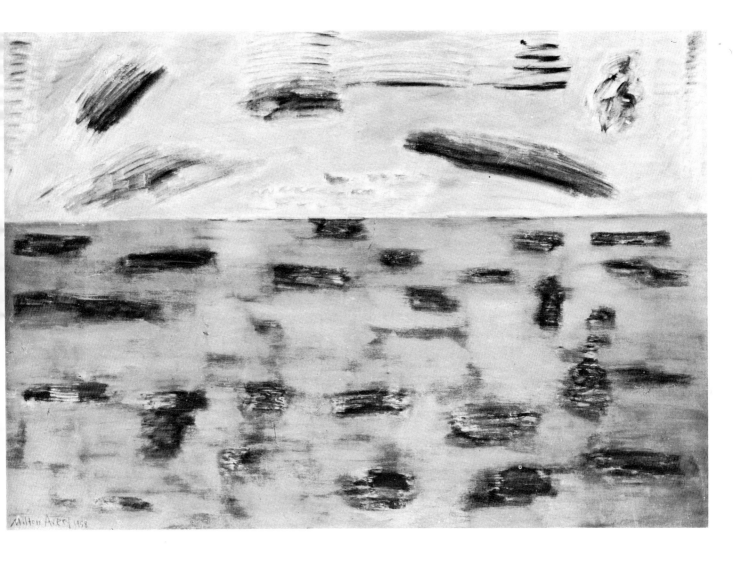

97 WHITE GULL, 1958

oil, 40 x 50
Lent by The Waddington Galleries

98 BLACK SEA, 1959

oil, 50 x 58
Lent by The Phillips Collection

99 FLIGHT, 1959
oil, 40 x 50
Lent by Dr. and Mrs. Hilbert H. DeLawter

100 SAND, SEA AND SKY, 1959
oil, 56 x 70
Lent by Larivière Collection

101 SPRING ORCHARD, 1959

oil, 50 x 66
Lent by National Collection of Fine Arts,
Smithsonian Institution,
S. C. Johnson Collection

102 TANGERINE MOON AND WINE DARK SEA,1959

oil, 60 x 72
Lent by Mr. and Mrs. David Lloyd Kreeger

103 BATHERS BY THE SEA, 1960

oil, 50 x 72
Lent anonymously

104 BEACH BLANKETS, 1960
oil, 54 x 72
Lent by Mr. and Mrs. S. O. Beren

105 BLUE BAY, 1960
oil, 50 x 60
Lent by Mr. and Mrs. Alex Bernstein

106 DUNES AND SEA II, 1960

oil, 52 x 72
Lent by Grace Borgenicht Gallery, Inc.

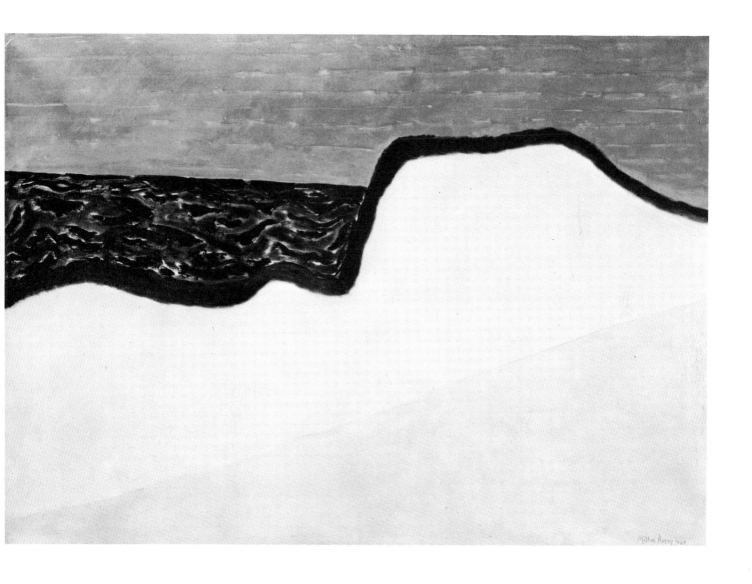

107 LONE GOAT, 1960
oil, 22 x 28
Lent anonymously

108 MEDITATION, 1960
oil, 68 x 40
Lent by Edward Albee
(exhibited in Washington and Brooklyn only)

09 MOUNTAIN LAKE, 1960
oil, 60 x 68
Lent by Grace Borgenicht Gallery, Inc.

110 MOUNTAIN AND MEADOW, 1960

oil, 60 x 68
Lent by Woodward Foundation

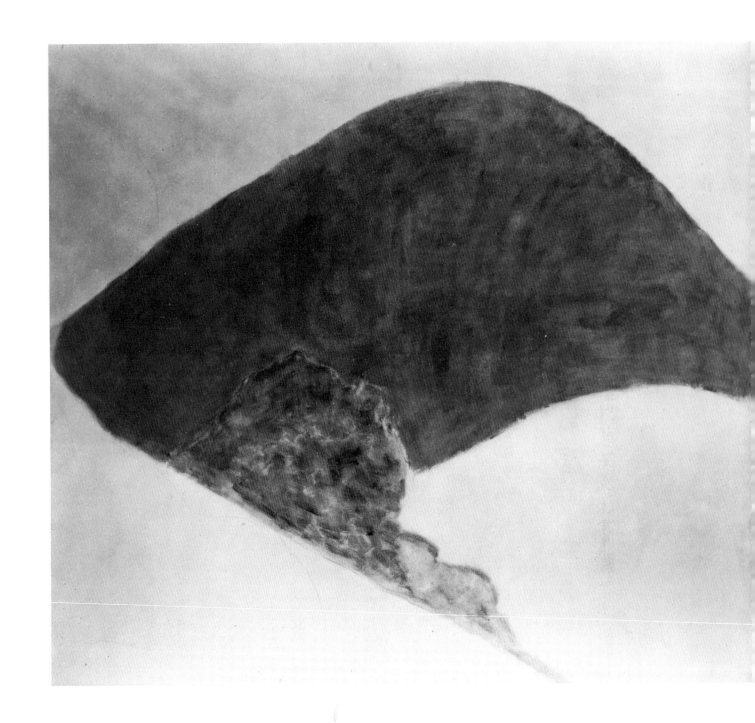

111 PLUNGING GULL, 1960

oil, 30 x 40
Lent by Mr. and Mrs. Jerome A. Friedland

112 ROBED NUDE, 1960
oil, 68 x 58
Lent by Dr. and Mrs. Sidney Merians

113 SEA BIRDS ON SAND BAR, 1960
   oil, 34 x 54
   Lent anonymously

114 SEA AND DUNES, 1960
   ink and pencil, 8½ x 11
   Lent by Mrs Milton Avery

115 YELLOW ROBE, 1960
oil, 60 x 50
Lent by Donald Morris Gallery, Inc.

116 YELLOW SAILFISH, 1960
   oil, 34 x 54
   Lent by Donald Morris Gallery, Inc

117 MILTON AVERY, 1961

oil, 42 x 30
Lent by Mrs. Milton Avery

118 NUDE COMBING HAIR, 1961

    drypoint, 8⅝ x 6⅛
    Lent by Associated American Artists

119 RUSHING SEA, 1961

    oil on canvas board, 22 x 30
    Lent by Mr. and Mrs. Donald Morris

120 DARK MOUNTAIN, LIGHT MOUNTAIN, 1962
oil on paper, 23 x 35
Lent by Grace Borgenicht Gallery, Inc.

121 DARK TREES, PALE MOUNTAIN, 1962
oil on paper, 23 x 35
Lent by Grace Borgenicht Gallery, Inc

122 DUNE GRASSES AND QUIET SEA, 1962
oil, 28 x 40
Lent by Mr. and Mrs. Philip G. Cavanaugh

123 SELF PORTRAIT, 1962

oil on paper, 23 x 18
Lent by Mr. and Mrs. Warren Brandt

124 TWO POETS, 1963

oil, 50 x 60
Lent anonymously

125 WHITE NUDE No. 2, 1963

    oil, 50 x 40
    Lent by Grace Borgenicht Gallery, Inc

126 WOMAN WITH GREEN FACE, 19

    oil, 23 x 23½
    Lent by Mr. and Mrs. Bernard Livingston
    (not reproduced)

127 THREE BIRDS, 1952

    woodcut, 9⅝ x 25
    Lent by Donald Morris Gallery, Inc.
    (not reproduced)

BIOGRAPHICAL NOTES

1893 Born in Altmar, New York, March 7.

1905 Avery family moved to Hartford, Connecticut.

1912 About this time, took a correspondence course in lettering.

1913 Worked the night shift at the United States Tire and Rubber Company in Hartford; spent the days painting in the countryside around the city.

1923 Studied one term, under Charles Noel Flagg, at the Connecticut League of Art Students.

1925 Summered in Gloucester, Massachusetts. In the fall, moved residence to New York, N.Y.

1926 Married Sally Michel, painter and illustrator.

1928 First exhibition (at the Opportunity Gallery, New York).

1929 Awarded Atheneum Prize by the Connecticut Academy of Fine Arts for an oil painting (now lost), *Brooklyn Bridge.*

1931 Awarded the Mr. and Mrs. Frank G. Logan Prize by the Art Institute of Chicago for *The White House* exhibited in the Institute's *11th International Water Color Exhibition.*

1932 Daughter March was born.

1933 Began working with drypoint plates.

1934 First museum purchase of an Avery made by the Phillips Collection, Washington, D.C. (*Harbor at Night,* no. 5).

1935 First one-man exhibition (at the Valentine Gallery, New York). From this time, work was frequently exhibited in one-man and group shows by many museums and commercial galleries in the United States and Europe. Summered in Vermont.

1936 Summered in Vermont.

1938 Summered on Gaspé Peninsula, Canada.

1941 Summered in California.

1943– Represented in New York by the dealers Rosenberg &
1950 Company, and Durand-Ruel Gallery.

1946 Summered in Mexico.

1947 Summered in the Canadian Northwest.

1948 Awarded first prize for *Sea and Rocks* exhibited in
The Baltimore National Water Color Exhibition, co-sponsored
by the Baltimore Museum of Art and Baltimore Water Color
Club.
Summered in Maine.

1950 Wintered in Florida.

1951 Began association with Grace Borgenicht Gallery, New York.
Wintered in Florida.

1952 First trip to Europe made in the summer; visited Paris
and the Riviera.

1954 Summered in New Hampshire.

1958 Awarded second prize in the exhibition sponsored by
the Boston Arts Festival.

1959 Awarded "Art USA 1959" prize for *Sea and Dune* 1 [no. 94].
Wintered in Florida.

1960 Major retrospective exhibition, organized and circulated by
the American Federation of Arts under a Ford Foundation
grant, opened at the Whitney Museum of American Art in
New York.
Wintered in Florida.

1965 Died in New York, January 3.

ELECTED REFERENCES

BOOKS AND PERIODICALS

arber, Manny. "Chaim Gross, Milton Avery, William Steig." *Magazine of Art,* vol. 36 (January 1943), pp. 10-15.

rost, Rosamund. "Milton Avery, American Fauve." *Art News,* vol. 41, (December 15, 1942), p. 28.

eldzahler, Henry. *American Painting in the Twentieth Century.* New York, 1965, pp. 172-173, 209.

reenberg, Clement. *Art and Culture: Critical Essays.* Boston, 1961, pp. 197-202.

──────────. "Milton Avery." *Arts,* vol. 32 (December 1957), pp. 40-45.

uest, Barbara. "Avery and Gatch: Lonely Americans." *Art News,* vol. 59 (March 1960), pp. 42-45.

ohnson, Una E. *Milton Avery Prints and Drawings 1930-1964.* Brooklyn, 1966.

ramer, Hilton. *Milton Avery: Paintings 1930-1960.* New York, 1962.

ouchheim, Aline B. "Double Perspective on Milton Avery." *Art News,* vol. 43 (January 15-31, 1945), p. 24.

Mellow, James R. "A Note on Milton Avery." *Art International,* vol. 12, (October 20, 1968), pp. 62-64.

Milton Avery Exhibition." *Baltimore Museum of Art News,* vol. 16 (December 1952-January 1953), pp. 7-9.

Milton Avery 1893-1965." *Arts,* vol. 39 (January 1965), p. 4.

Moore, Barbara. In Lee Nordness [ed.], *Art USA Now,* Lucerne, Switzerland, 1962, pp. 66-68.

Morsell, Mary. "Milton Avery." *Art News,* vol. 33 (March 16, 1935), p. 14.

Mullins, Edwin. "Developments in Style XV: Milton Avery." *The London Magazine,* vol. 4 (January 1965), pp. 34-40.

Munro, Eleanor C. "Solitary, pale, and peaceable." *Art News,* vol. 55 (April 1956), pp. 25, 95.

Printmaking: A Family Affair." *Artist's Proof,* V, vol. 3 (Spring-Summer, 1963), p. 29.

Riley, Maude. "Milton Avery Fills an International Gap." *The Art Digest,* vol. 19 (January 15, 1945), p. 10.

Ritter, Chris. "A Milton Avery Profile." *The Art Digest,* vol. 27 (December 1, 1952), pp. 11-12, 22.

Salpeter, Harry. "Art Career in Two Keys." *Esquire* (July, 1945), pp. 72-73, 160-162.

Seckler, Dorothy Gees. "A Very Nice Avery." *Art News,* vol. 51 (December 1952), pp. 30-31, 60-61.

Swenson, May. "Milton Avery." *Arts Yearbook,* vol. 3 (1959), pp. 108-113.

Wolf, Ben. "Twin Avery Shows." *Art Digest,* vol. 20 (February 1, 1946), p. 13.

II EXHIBITION CATALOGUES

"My Daughter, March" by Milton Avery. Durand-Ruel Gallery, New York, 1947.

Milton Avery. Baltimore Museum of Art, 1952; essay by Frederick S. Wight.

Milton Avery. Museum of Fine Arts of Houston, 1956; statement by the artist.

Milton Avery. Felix Landau Gallery, Los Angeles, 1956.

Milton Avery. The American Federation of Arts, New York, 1960; essay by Adelyn D. Breeskin.

Paintings by Milton Avery. Park Gallery, Detroit, 1962.

Milton Avery. The Waddington Galleries, London, England, 1962; essay by Clement Greenberg.

Milton Avery, Etchings and Woodcuts. Associated American Artists, New York, 1963.

Milton Avery. Donald Morris Gallery, Detroit, 1964.

Milton Avery. The Waddington Galleries, London, England, 1965.

Milton Avery Paintings 1941-1963. Museum of Modern Art, New York, 1965-1966.

Milton Avery 1893-1965. Richard Gray Gallery, Chicago, 1966.

Milton Avery 1893-1965. Sheldon Memorial Art Gallery, University of Nebraska, Lincoln, and The Arkansas Art Center, Little Rock, 1966.

Milton Avery Middle Period Paintings: 1935-1953. The Waddington Galleries, London, England, 1967.

Milton Avery. Grace Borgenicht Gallery, New York, 1968.

The Neuberger Collection, An American Collection, Paintings, Drawings, and Sculpture. Museum of Art, Rhode Island School of Design, Providence, 1968.

Milton Avery 1893-1965. Gallery Reese Palley, San Francisco, 1968.